The Dynamics of Global Leadership

Acknowledgement

I want to acknowledge Chris Johnson whose imaginative genius created this and previous book covers; whose kind feedback has dramatically improved my communication skills; whose ability to understand and relate to how I think has helped me believe in myself more; and whose friendship is of inestimable value in my life.

I wouldn't be where I am today without the talent, support and friendship of Chris.

DEDICATION

This book is dedicated to everyone who followed their heart and inspiration when there was little or no support for doing so. You are the true heroes on Earth.

TABLE OF CONTENTS

Forward

The best thing we can do for our self is to be honest with our self, and the worst thing is to lie to our self.

An important of being honest with our self is to accept our true potential. One important part of accepting our ability is accepting we have the ability, without any cooperation from anyone else, to experience all the love, joy and peace that exists.

To the degree we demonstrate that ability, we inspire others to access that same ability within themselves. Nothing could ever change the world more dramatically than that.

Introduction

The solution to every problem is a greater acceptance of the truth.

We have problems in the world today and they will be solved by a greater acceptance of the truth. While there is disagreement among many of what the truth is and what is most important to focus our attention on right now, an honest commitment to a greater acceptance and alignment with the truth will resolve all these conflicts.

I believe, deep down, we all know what is true. As you read this book, pay attention to what resonates deeply within you and ask yourself, is this true for me. I promise if you do this, this book will both change your life and you will change the world for the better.

Part of being honest right now is accepting that **I, you and everyone else have the power to change our self and the world in real, practical, visible and powerfully beneficial ways.**

Chapter 1

The Need for Global Conscious Leadership

At this writing there is a strong sentiment that the way to thrive is to become more of an isolationist focused on our own short-term immediate welfare, as we see it. There is a denial of the fact among that segment of the world's population that we all impact each other. If one group or nation is suffering it causes us all problems. Radiation from a nuclear disaster spreads worldwide. The oceans touch every continent. The more international trade, the stronger the economy of every country is. **The more communication between those of different races, religions, countries and cultures, the safer and more secure we all are.**

We need global leadership that understands and can communicate there are win/win solutions to our individual and global problems. We need leaders who have made that practical in their own lives to serve as inspiring examples. We need leaders who put accepting and aligning with the truth ahead of being right; whose warmth, compassion and wisdom can resonate the warmth, compassion and wisdom in others.

At this moment in history, as in every other moment in history, we have the challenge to move our society and the world forward; to dramatically increase the expression of peace, love and joy in the world. **The power to increase**

our experience, individually and collectively, of love, joy and peace is the only power worth having. We only want money, power, land, fame, influence, and possessions because we believe they will increase our experience of love, joy and peace. The truth is love, joy and peace can exist with or without these things. These things may or may not come into our life as our experience of more love, joy and peace grows; AND the more love, joy and peace we have, the less we care about anything else because **love, joy and peace contain all the value that exists.**

We need global leadership that is an example of living with love, joy and peace; leadership who acts consistent with love, joy and peace; leaders who are adept at identifying and implementing win/win solutions that lift everyone up. That is the global conscious leadership we need now, and at every other time as well.

Chapter 2

The True Source of Global Power

All power, including global power, has the acceptance of truth at its core. Only when we can accept the truth about our self can we see clearly the truth in the outer world. The reason the United States is the most powerful country in the world is because we find value in all cultures and religions and provide a structure for all of us to work together for our individual and common good. Yes, there is plenty of room for improvement and there is a reason that so many people who could choose to live anywhere in the world choose to live in the United States.

Seeing our self in others, accepting our own and other's value, are big and important aspects of accepting what is true; the ultimate source of power.

All people have worth and value. When we accept and act on that truth our power grows immensely. **We are stronger when we accept the truth that when we help or hurt others, we are simultaneously helping or hurting our self.**

The greatest and most powerful and successful of all leaders have had the clarity to communicate in various degrees of effectiveness that co cooperating for our common good is best for us individually and collectively. Their power comes from an acceptance of the fact we are all one. Their effectiveness comes from their ability to translate that wisdom into constructive behavior that people relate to as benefitting themselves and others. We don't have to be global or even community leaders to experience all the power that exists. We need only accept the truth of who and what we are; simple but by no means easy.

Chapter 3

Making Transition

A great many of us have been focused on our careers, money, our family and our physical health. As we grow in our personal honesty we increasingly come to understand the benefits of all those pursuits are maximized when we focus on a deeper acceptance of the truth.

It's not that I don't care for and take care of my family, or get mortgages for my clients; I do. In fact, I do it better than ever. The difference is how I view it all. When I get a loan for a client, I no longer see it as an opportunity to earn money, even though I do earn money. I no longer see it as an opportunity to help someone, although I do help people. I see it as an opportunity to experience more deeply the love I am. From that state I find myself congruently telling clients I'll do all I can to help them. That isn't said for effect or even because I believe in helping people. It's a spontaneous expression of the love I am.

Making the transition from viewing and thinking about our actions as an effort to create a result to viewing and thinking about our behavior as an honest expression of our acceptance of who we are, makes all the difference in the world. Some of the most important differences in transitioning from acting to achieve to acting as a spontaneous expression of who are include: more control over our life, greater peace of mind, a dramatic increase in our influence on others, improved health and vitality, greater business success and the list goes on and on. **The biggest impact we can have in the outer world is deeply inspiring others to follow our example of always looking to accept the truth more fully. This is global leadership at its finest.**

Having read this, the truth of it will come up in your mind more and more. More and more you will come to understand how effective and practical it is to focus on truth. A big piece of accepting what is true is realizing that focusing on "being our self" is the most beneficial and productive thing we can do.

Truth is a force constantly working to make itself known. We can thrive by willingly accepting and aligning with it more fully, or destroy our self by resisting it. Ultimately the truth is stronger than any resistance to hide or destroy it. The truth eventually comes out.

As we're more honest with our self, we more honestly accept that how we view our self, the world and our place in it has a global impact. The more honest we are with our self the more dramatically we inspire the whole world, and the more fully we accept and relate to this being true.

Our positive impact on our own life, the lives of those we love, the lives of our friends and clients, and in fact the lives of all inhabitants in the world is maximized by us accepting and being our self at the deepest levels we can achieve.

I know all the wisdom and love that exists, exists within each of us, including me. I know the degree to which I can accept and align with the love and wisdom I am, I will inspire others to accept and align with the love and wisdom they are. There is a level of self acceptance available to each of us that is so powerful it inspires and is effective at supporting those throughout the world to accept and relate to the love, wisdom and wholeness they are. I don't yet have that level of self-acceptance, and I'm moving closer to it all the time. All I, or anyone else, need ever do to grow in our love, wisdom and power is to be continually focused on accepting what is true at continually deeper levels.

Chapter 4

Acknowledging a Variety of Individual Development

We're all in different places in our lives and development. It's not better or worse to be a child or an adult. It's not better or worse to be a beginner or an advanced soul in our spiritual development. The truth is, we are where we are in life. We have the level of health, joy, happiness and peace we have right now. There is great value in honestly accepting where we are.

For me, I'm still learning AND I've already learned a great deal that is valuable to share. It's important for my own well being I accept both are true. Because I understand and accept that some things I know and am accomplished at and some things I've yet to learn and master, allows me to relate to others and see myself in them. It is as wasteful to try to teach a newborn to drive a car as it is to try to teach an engineer basic arithmetic. We need to address our self and others where we are now.

What is true is that there is a "next step" forward for every individual. We all have the opportunity to grow and improve our lives. As global leaders we are challenged to see our self in people in all stages of development, to relate to them and their perspectives, to "get" them, and be able to beneficially communicate wit them. We might share the wonder of discovery with a baby; the healing of acceptance and self forgiveness with a parent preparing to pass on; the anger and frustration of those not happy with their lives and the opportunities they don't believe are available to them; the fear of those petrified to move forward in their lives; the joy of those growing and accomplishing; and the list goes on for ever. **The more we relate to and see our self in others, the grater clarity we have in how to share a deeper acceptance of our self in a way that benefits us and them.**

Using our ability to recognize and relate to different levels of development in others, affords us the opportunity to deepen our own development and lift others up by example. I had a friend going through tough times. I shared with him a time when I had a goal to make it through the next 3 minutes. That's how much stress I was under. Sharing that story strengthened my belief in my ability to respond effectively to the most difficult and stressful situations and also inspired hope in my friend. I have another friend looking to find greater focus in his life. I shared my focus and how I strengthen it to give him ideas and it also improved my focus. There is always an opportunity to lift our self and others up. We can build our ability at recognizing and capitalizing on these opportunities through practice.

No matter what stage of development someone is in, we have the ability to see our self in them and respond constructively for all. Our example changes the world.

Chapter 5

Responding to Resistance

More fully accepting what's true and dealing with things as they are can be perceived as being painful and something to be avoided. That's why so many people procrastinate in doing their taxes. That's how people get hooked on drugs. That's why some people over eat and drink too much. Accepting the reality of truth can be frightening and something many of us want to avoid. As someone who has been, and to some extent still is, afraid every day, I can relate to not wanting to address certain things in my life.

If we're to be effective at responding to resistance in others, we must first become more adept at responding to our own resistance.

What works best for me in overcoming my resistance is to first accept its existence. I am resistant to taking on the responsibilities I associate with having a large following; a lot of clients; a deep impact on other's thinking and behavior. Next, I do my best to honestly assess the situation. No-one is going to follow or employ me unless they feel it's in their own interests to do so, and that's solely their choice. Further, I believe in the value of what I have to share. Thirdly, the value to me is that by sharing what I have to say I am allowing my belief in myself to gain acceptance and that is the greatest gift I can give myself and others. Lastly, I come to a place where I tell myself I deserve to give myself the opportunity to try, and resolve to go forward. That's how I respond to resistance within myself. Having done that, I'm much better able to relate to and help others having similar issues.

All of us have resistance and each of us benefits from having a process that works for us to beneficially respond to that resistance. The better example we are of responding effectively to resistance, the more we inspire and support others to do the same.

As global leaders we must be effective at responding effectively to resistance, ours and others. **The more we see our self in others, the more effectively we can communicate with them.**

Chapter 6

An Optimal Level of Structure

For this world to thrive we must honestly accept people have a wide range of development. We have people "right of the turnip truck" (new souls), old souls, injured souls, bright light souls; a big variety.

There is an optimal level of structure for any given individual and in fact every area of endeavor for each individual. Someone may need a lot of guidance in one area and be completely accomplished in another. Some people need to be in jail to prevent them from doing more damage to themselves and others while others would do the right thing even if there were no laws.

The more we grow, the more we provide our own structure and the less support we require from outer structure. When I was a child, I needed the structure of the school system. As a self-employed adult I decide what I want to learn when, how I spend my time, how I behave towards others and what I do and don't do.

By understanding and providing the optimal levels of structure for people in various areas of their life, the growth of individuals and society is optimized. While we are unlikely to ever get it perfect, **understanding different people need different levels of support and structure in different parts of their life we create a far more effective, compassionate and successful society.**

Chapter 7

Our Part

We each have a role to play in making the world whatever it is. The more we focus on our own growth and development, the more positive contribution we make to the world automatically.

Sadly, I've seen so much effort expended by **people trying to make a positive contribution to the world that would have had such greater impact if only those people worked on themselves more.** We can't give what we don't have and **our greatest impact is our example.** If we wish to help lift up others, we have to be an example of lifting our selves up. If we want others to "see the light" and change their ways for the better, we need to "see the light" and change our ways for the better. If we want people to be kinder and more loving, we need to be kinder and more loving. If we want people to be wiser and more aware of cause and effect in the their lives, we need to be an example of that.

In writing this book I am growing in my willingness to trust my heart and follow my inspiration. My example will inspire others to follow their heart and trust in their inspiration more. That's how real leadership works.

If we're putting maximum effort into being the best person we can be, we're doing our part. That means always be honest with our self, kinder and more supportive of our selves and others. **It's true that whenever we lift someone else up, we are lifted up and whenever we lift** our selves up, everyone else is lifted up as well. We are one.

Chapter 8

What Happens if We Don't Have Conscious Global Leadership

Without conscious global leadership decisions are no longer made with the understanding that the means is the end. People justify hurting and killing others. They convince themselves of the lie they can get ahead by defeating or even killing others. Nations become more isolationist focusing on trying to "protect our own" rather than realizing true security comes from mutually beneficial relationships and trading.

Without conscious leadership terrorism grows. With conscious leadership we understand the cause of terrorism is people believing they will be better off if they destroy others. We can shine light on the fact that isn't true. **As long as people lie to themselves by convincing themselves their lack of love, joy and peace are caused by others, they'll do anything they can to eliminate those they feel are depriving them of the love, joy and peace they desire.** It's not just terrorists that blame others for the problems in their lives. Republicans and Democrats blame each other, management and labor blame each other, the rich and poor blame each other, and many husbands and wives blame each other.

Without conscious leadership we devolve into increasingly blaming others for our problems and the problems of the world. The more we see others as the enemy the less cooperation and the worse life is for us all.

In politics today it's easy to see the venom, the lies and the blame. That's all due to unconscious leadership. Truth brings awareness and focus to the fact we all rise or fall together. As such, truth promotes cooperation, having honest discussions aimed at defining the optimal path forward (not being "right"), trust and respect.

Unconscious leadership leads to seeing everyone as the enemy, fear, isolation and war. Conscious leadership leads to cooperation, trust, mutual benefit, acknowledgement of interdependence and peace.

Chapter 9

What the Changes You Make Mean for You Personally and Those You Care About

As individuals we can choose to look for, create and participate in activities that are mutually beneficial, win win. Or, we can focus more of our attention in trying to protect what we have from others, assuming others will try to do their worst to us and try to defend our self from the anticipated attack.

There's a reason why over 95% of marriages with premarital agreements don't last 5 years. The focus is on defending assets, not maximizing love and trust. Personally, I wouldn't marry anyone I thought I needed a premarital agreement with.

Without trust we can't buy or do much of anything. We build trust by seeing our self in others. If I recognize in you the same commitment to do the right thing I see in myself, it's far easier for me to trust you. This is as true for nations (just a lot of people) as it is for individuals.

The stronger we are, the more clarity we have, the more effectively we communicate; the more people we positively influence with our example . The more we operate from deeper perspectives the stronger we are and the further our influence reaches.

If in getting a mortgage for one of my clients, I see uploading documents to a lender as simply uploading documents it has one level of impact in the world. If I see it as serving my client it has a greater impact. If I see it as making the systems that were created to support people effective, it has a still greater positive impact. If I see it as **a loving act expressing care for myself and others resonating more love in the world**, it has even greater impact.

Our lives and the lives of others are immeasurably enriched when we relate to our behavior as a loving act that resonates with the love of others around the world. I believe that is positive effective global leadership.

Chapter 10

Resources We Can Draw Upon

We have both internal and external resources we can draw upon.

The more we see and value our internal resources and draw upon them the more we will recognize and be able to effectively avail ourselves of external resources.

One of our most valuable internal resources is our drive to improve our life. The more we relate to and accept that drive, the more energy and resilience we have. I'd do anything I thought would increase my experience of love, joy and peace in the world. That's why I meditate every day and have for over 35 years. That's why I act on my inspiration. That's why I put so much into getting my outer world to match my inner world. **With enough energy anyone can accomplish anything.** That energy comes from acknowledging our internal drive.

The more we support our self, the better we are at getting external support. I write a book and my friend designs the cover for me. I care for and serve my mortgage clients and they support me with their loyalty, spanning decades in many instances. I support myself by helping people in Toastmasters (when I help others I'm automatically helping myself as well). They support me with encouragement, creative ideas, mortgage business, friendship and marketing assistance.

We all have a vast array of resources within us and available to us in the world. I am always working on drawing more wisdom, kindness and compassion from deep inside myself and recognizing and benefitting from help and resources in the world. The more we focus on drawing effectively on our resources the better we get at it.

Chapter 11

Giving and Receiving Help

I always look to help in areas I want to strengthen within myself. As president of a Toastmasters club my objective was to strengthen my acceptance of my own worth and value. My strategy, which proved very effective, was to acknowledge the character strengths of those I introduced every week. I employed the fact that anytime I lift up another I'm automatically lifted up as well. It worked beautifully.

I want to improve my ability to turn concepts that uplift society into successful businesses with ever greater positive impact. I'm helping to coach and support someone else with the same objective. The detachment I have in working with him allows me greater clarity. Then all I need to do is take my own advice.

All real help is mutually beneficial. If people help me and it results in me earning money, I share the profits with them in addition to my appreciation.

Chapter 12

Act Now

Let's all commit to being more honest with our self and acting from a deeper perspective.

I'm going to look at my daily activities more and more as caring acts that resonate more love in the world. I am going to trust, act on, and value the wisdom I have more by publishing and promoting this book. I am going to be more open in sharing my understanding of the fact we are all one and how it affects my behavior and enriches my life.

What are you going to do?

Epilog

I want greater constructive involvement with you. I want your support and I want to support you in maximizing our growth and our contribution to the world.

Reach out to me at scott@visirity.com and let's be a shining example of how by combining forces we can dramatically improve our individual lives and the world at the same time.

Part of what I offer includes public speeches, corporate speeches, trade association speeches, corporate consulting, and political consulting. Introductions to those benefitting from what I have to offer are greatly appreciated.

www.ingramcontent.com/pod-product-compliance
Lightning Source LLC
Chambersburg PA
CBHW070243290526
45789CB00004B/1746